Grand Pa- Good news from the Good Feel Cornfield

Grand Pa- Good news from the Good Feel Cornfield

Grand Pa- Good news from the Good Feel Cornfield
ISBN: Softcover 978-1-955581-05-9
Copyright © 2021 by Charles Finney

All rights reserved. No part of this book may be reproduced or transmitted in any form or by any means, electronic or mechanical, including photocopying, recording, or by any information storage and retrieval system, without permission in writing from the publisher.

Parson's Porch Books is an imprint of Parson's Porch & Company (PP&C) in Cleveland, Tennessee. PP&C is an innovative organization which raises money by publishing books of noted authors, representing all genres. Its face and voice is **David Russell Tullock.**
(dtullock@parsonsporch.com).

Parson's Porch & Company *turns books into bread & milk* by sharing its profits with the poor.

www.parsonsporch.com

Contents

Grand Pa and the Cornfield 9
Grand Pa and the Corn Field Church 14
Grand Pa and the Chicken Nest 16
Grand Pa -The Voice of the IRS 20
Grandpa- The Doors 23
Grandpa and the Mule 27
Grand Pa and the Rats 30
Grand Pa and the Paint Brush 35
Grand Pa-Act Your Age 38
Grand Pa- The Cluttered Shed 42
Grand Pa and the Book 45
Grand Pa-All Washed Off 49
Grand Pa -The Quilt 52
Grand Pa , Baseball, and Dad 58
Grand Pa and the Gift 63
Grand Pa and the Angels 68
Grandpa-Words 72
Grandpa-The Snakes and the Birds 76
Grand Pa- The Farewell 80
Grandpa -Into the sunset 84

Grand Pa- Good news from the Good Feel Cornfield

There was always good news in and around the Cornfield. Good Feel news filled with homespun laughter within this southern country homestead, Biblical good news for all. Meet Grand Pa in the selected short articles with his commonsense approach to life, religion farming and people. Common sense and Biblical Scriptures joining for life lessons. Then there is Grand ma, learned woman with extra ordinary business skills. Of course, no one forgets distant cousin J.R. and all the things he has yet to do. The animals and critters also find a place to share the cornfield. Family farm fun awaits. Many country blessings for the reader. Come on in and shuck some corn. That is pull back the layers and find your kernel of blessing.

,

Grand Pa and the Cornfield

Grand Pa used to talk about his corn field as though it was a mystical place. It was a place that he loved to go when the corn was tall and full. The corn shucks being full green with golden tassels rising over six feet high above his head. They with their broad leaves full of corn providing a nice shade for Grand Pa to just go, sit and consider.

I often wondered what he was doing when I would see him disappear into the stalks of corn. So, one day, I followed him. Right to the middle of the cornfield. There he sat. In a place you could tell no corn was planted. The middle was so marked by a small cross. One side, painted red, facing the east. The other side painted white and facing west. Right at the cross, he sat. on the ground, dirty coveralls, and his blue green flannel shirt, looking upward..

So, I approached him quietly and asked him , "what you doing"? He replies, "just considering". Now Grandpa might not have a lot of book learning, but he had a lot of what they called common sense. I asked him "what was he considering?" He replied to me "What is there not to consider?" He said "well I have to think carefully about my crop. Is it growing right?. When will it be time to harvest? All things to consider. Then other times I sit and consider how I treat others and how they treat me in an attentive or kindly way. Sometimes I just sit and consider God. That's why there is a cross in the middle of my corn field. I come here to remind myself how he gave me the strength and health to plant the corn. How amazing his works of nature to send the right amount of rain and sunshine for the corn to grow. How he keeps the pest off the crop. . To simply gaze on his handiwork in making this cornfield grow. Some time I just sit and reflect or deliberate my purpose in life and if I am doing my best. Just considering...

Grand pa said, "Today we all need to sit and consider.". Consider HIM. Consider Joy. Consider Jesus. Consider the Lilies. Simply consider!. He said, "It seems like we as a nation no longer consider". The duties we owe to God, our family, our neighbors and to ourselves. We have failed to consider the journey of others and the roads they have had to travel. We have failed to consider the hardships and toils that has beset our world. The only thing we consider these day is if we can take a material thing to self-satisfy. We do not consider others.

Grand ma was reading me a magazine article that said, "Today in the USA alone, we have an estimated population of 331,002,651". Now that is a big number. He said I bet you cannot cipher that high. He said I usually sow about 100 plants of corn for a 50 ft row. If I had that many rows of corn, I bet I have enough to go to the moon. I could feed the world.

He said, "It's amazing, but no matter how hard I try, I can't seem to plow two rows of corn the same". In essence, that is the same with people, Consider, there is that many rows of corn. The plants are always side by side, but never together. They are apart as I planted so they can grow and expand to deliver a harvest.

Some people on the other hand are also apart. Without joining together, they feel alone and get depressed. They trod and labor, but don't bloom and harvest. Some are planted and seek an interconnection thru Church, family, friends, hobbies, work, and even political considerations. They tend to grow when the soil they are planted in is rich and nourished. Those people have a value of self-worth, Few if any weeds of deception are about them But there are others whose soil is not rich and is loosely nourished and they are not connected and feel no self-worth. They tend to get lost in the weeds.. They simply are working, but not considering. Haggai 1:5 *Now therefore thus saith the LORD of hosts; Consider your ways.*

I know that if the corn seed falls out of the planting spot, that the crows will swoop down and eat it. There will be no corn harvest from those seeds. It seems like today too many seeds have fallen on top of the ground. People have failed to consider the consequences of the separation of the principles of truth and morality. People have failed to show grace and no longer know grace. Our dereliction of duty has led us to not a nation under God, but to a nation apart from God. People have abandoned God, and in their self-wisdom believe that the loose seeds on top of the ground will grow and be a harvest. They don't even consider the hungry crow or any deception that may forgo them. People must ask themselves of God "Are we to consider ourselves as his people?" Exo 33:13 *Now therefore, I pray thee, if I have found grace in thy sight, shew me now thy way, that I may know thee, that I may find grace in thy sight: and consider that this nation is thy people.*

We need to return to a day of consideration. Deut 4:39 *Know therefore this day, and consider it in thine heart, that the LORD he is God in heaven above, and upon the earth beneath: there is none else.* We need to consider that God is a God of mercy and love, but there will come a day when he will judge and chasteneth you. Deut 8:5 *Thou shalt also consider in thine heart, that, as a man chasteneth his son, so the LORD thy God chasteneth thee.*

Consider things past. Deut 32:7 *Remember the days of old, consider the years of many generations: ask thy father, and he will shew thee; thy elders, and they will tell thee.* The time we have to exist must be considered. Not only the past, or even the present, but for the latter time. Deut 32:29 *O that they were wise, that they understood this, that they would consider their latter end!*

Consider Jesus. Consider his death upon a cross. Consider His Resurrection, but more importantly consider His Return. Consider if you are ready for His return. 1 Sam 12:24 *Only fear the LORD and serve him in truth with all your heart: for consider how great things he hath done for you. He* loved you so much He died for your sins. But even greater is His love, as daily He blesses each of us. He hears and answers prayers. 7.8 billion prayers in the world daily if they pray with a sincere heart.

Psa 8:3 *When I consider thy heavens, the work of thy fingers, the moon, and the stars, which thou hast ordained;* Consider the majesty and beauty of the world He created. Consider the failing of man as he polluted and daily destroys it.

Eccles 7:14 *In the day of prosperity be joyful, but in the day of adversity consider God also hath set the one over against the other, to the end that man should find nothing after him.*

2 Tim 2:7 *Consider what I say, and the Lord give thee understanding in all things.*

Hebrews 10:24 *And let us consider one another to provoke unto love and to good works:*

Consider this day! Consider someone else!

Grand Pa and the Corn Field Church

Grandpa was not what you might call a religious man. He did tell me once how he thought about the hereafter. He said, "since I have gotten older, "No matter where I am - in the living room, bedroom, in the kitchen, or out at the barn, I am always asking myself: 'Now, what am I here after?'" Now Grandpa was a man that believed in giving his ten percent. He once gave a tithe of more than ten percent. He gave of his farmland. He gave ,at no charge, about 10 acres. being what he said was his best cornfield. to a local congregation to build a church. The land being creek feed, he said his harvest of corn on that part of the farm was not bad. But he hoped the Church would bring in a new crop of folks for Grandma to socialize with.. And if they wanted they could use the creek for baptizing. His closest neighbor and his wife were over a mile away.

Now, Grandpa did not always go inside the church. Some of the church folks could see him sitting under a shade tree outside the building. He would be their head bowed, listening to the preacher and the choir. When I asked him why he would sit under the tree, he replied "I don't always know God is inside the building, but out here under the tree

He shows me all his wonderful works. He lets me see Him in nature. Beside the choir would sometimes sing off key and my chickens could cackle better than them, But the birds outside, never missed a note, how beautiful they would sing. I remember Grandma reading me the Bible in Psalm 104-2 *By them shall the fowls of the heaven have their habitation, which sing among the branches.* God sends special birds each Sunday just to sing for me,.

But one Sunday, there was no birds. He said "So I decided to go inside the church. There I meet a man. Not in a physical sense, but I could feel His presence inside me. Then I prayed to God, and He accepted me, and I accepted Him. Job 33-26 *He shall pray unto God, and he will be favorable unto him: and he shall see his face with joy: for he will render unto man his righteousness. 27 He looketh upon men, and if any say, I have sinned, and perverted that which was right, and it profited me not; 28 He will deliver his soul from going into the pit, and his life shall see the light.* Grandpa got baptized in the creek.

The last time my Grand Pa was inside the church was at his funeral. A light shown through a window near his casket. Birds were singing. Romans 12-15 *Rejoice with those who rejoice, and weep with those who weep.16 Be of the same mind toward one another. Do not set your mind on high things, but associate with the humble. Do not be wise in your own opinion.* Grandpa's last thoughts on his old cornfield was "You know on a good year I might get 40 bushel of corn an acre over there. Just think, now they are harvesting more than 50 believers a year that come to know Jesus as their personal Savior,. The preaching not to bad and best of all the birds sing harmoniously with the choir. Psalm 1-3 *And he shall be like a tree planted by the rivers of water, that bringeth forth his fruit in his season; his leaf also shall not wither; and whatsoever he doeth shall prosper.* What's planted in your cornfield?

Grand Pa and the Chicken Nest

Grand Pa was not a man of very many words. His vocabulary was not strong as he never went to school. He could not read or write, But one day, I noticed a sign over the side of the barn where Grand ma kept her laying hens. The sign said "Nidification". The sign was tattered and worn. You could tell it was older than the barn .Being at a lost as to the meaning of the word and wondering why Grand pa would put up a sign like this was puzzling, so I asked him. He said "years ago I was a deck hand in the Merchant Marines. We went to Italy to unload some cargo. While at the dock, I found an old man making Bird Houses. I asked him how much for one. He looked puzzled at me as he could speak no English. Worse, I could not speak Latin or any other foreign language. I only spoke good old southern country redneck slang. I pointed at the bird house, and he pointed at a sign that said Nidification. Soon, together we understood that I wanted to buy a bird house.

So, with a big smile he said " Nidification". I nodded yes. He was a kind man. After I paid him for the bird house, he gave me his bird house selling sign too. A ship mate told me later that this was Latin in origin and means "to build a nest. "He said now Nidicolous is used to mean "living in a nest."

Grand Pa told me. you know a nest is a place of rest, retreat, or lodging. In other words, a home, a place of refuge.Nests are built using several different types of materials. They are placed in various places to provide shelter, safety, warmth, and protection. Many animals seek natural cavities in the ground or in trees to build their nests. Each nest is a labor of love and commitment. So are the nests your Grandma laying hens are in. She took real care in making them exactly right for her chickens. So, I hung my bird building sign so the chickens would know where their nests were. I figured it was the right thing to do as most of those chickens were not local hens, but so foreign that came from nearly twenty miles away. You could tell, they cackled differently.

Grandpa said you know one day after sitting under my favorite shade tree, I thought we Humans also build a nest, but we call it a house. Like all animals that build a nest, we gather our favorite things around us to create a safe dwelling place providing us warmth, comfort, security, beauty, and peace. Each of our homes is unique to us. They reflect our personality, our passions, interests, and family life. We build our nest to make it our home. While your Grand ma and my house was not filled with lots of material things, it was filled with love and laughter with all seven kids.

Grand Pa said after a while looking at the new church in his old cornfield, I realized that it too was a sort of a nest. Today's church house is like a nest. A place of rest, retreat, and refuge from the World. They are built by different denominations united in the adherence of their beliefs and practices. They offer a place for believers to praise, give thanks, worship, sing, reflect and rest with the Creator. Although they may differ in doctrine, all churches are held together not by brick and mortar but by a body of writings considered sacred. The **Scriptures**..

2 Timothy 3:16 *"All scripture is given by inspiration of God, and is profitable for doctrine, for reproof, for correction, for instruction in righteousness:"*

.Grandpa said there is the mystery of the church as a nest. "It is not a building. It's a people, with or without a building. A nest united with a labor of brotherly love and commitment. It has a builder, and the builder is the Christ, the Son of the living God. Jesus builds the church. The place where love, grace, and mercy dwells. When we belong to Christ, we nest and dwell.

Psalm 18:4 *One thing have I desired of the LORD, that will I seek after; that I may **dwell in** the house of the LORD all the days of my life, to behold the beauty of the LORD, and to inquire in his temple.*

The nest or church is a place of peace and brotherly love. It is built upon the confession of Jesus as God's Son and Christ .The church is engaged in persuading unbelievers to become disciples of Jesus which the Great Commission defines as baptizing them and teaching them to obey Christ.

John 13:34 *A new commandment I give unto you, That ye love one another; as I have loved you, that ye also love one another.* **35** *By this shall all men know that ye are my disciples, if ye have love one to another.*

Psalm 91:2 *I will say of the LORD, He is my refuge and my fortress: my God; in him will I trust*

We all are welcomed to enter the refuge, a sinner. With the stirring of our hearts and upon our confession and belief of Jesus as God's son and Christ, we are filled and saved with peace, joy, love, and forgiveness. The church is successful in

Nidification. Its nest grows when people show love one to another. Its members like my chickens have a safe place to roost.

Psalm 84-3 Y*ea, the sparrow hath found a house, and the swallow a nest for herself, where she may lay her young, even thine altars, O LORD of hosts, my King, and my God. 4 Blessed are they that dwell in thy house: they will be still praising thee.*

Find a church, nest, and build on its foundation. Share love to cushion the hardships of others. Be blessed and praise the Lord ..

Grand Pa - The Voice of the IRS

Grand Pa would do anything he could to please Grand ma. He would, when he had the money, buy her anything she wanted. Grand pa always said he did not mind paying taxes on things he bought, but he did mind on what the government men spent it on. If he did not have the money, he tried to please her with household chores. Then on one colorful autumn night, Grand ma came to him and said I need some laying hens and a rooster.

Well Grand pa went about the other farmers, then to the local farmers co-op and got Grand ma some fine laying hens. Grand pa used to say, "Listen to that sweet cackle sound. Those hens are laying eggs for my breakfast tomorrow. The rooster he got Grand ma was a fine bird. The only thing wrong with it was its voice. It had none. A sweet cock a doodle do was all he could muster. Grand ma said that bird could not wake up the hens to start their laying.

Grand Pa told Grand ma, let's wait till spring to see if the rooster voice improves. If not then you decide. So Grand ma did the only thing possible that early Spring.. She got another rooster. What they called a banty rooster. Half the size of Grand Pa rooster but with a voice loud enough to wake up the few people buried in a cemetery just a mile down the road.

Grand ma told Grand pa, just you watch them hens get up early now. They will be up so early laying eggs that tomorrow morning you may get a double portion. Grand ma said, "just you listen and watch". The next morning that banty rooster crowed so loud and with an irritating crackle. Every hen laid four eggs. Now most hens lay five or six in a week. But four in one night! The sound of the little rooster made all the difference.

Well mid-April was approaching and even though Grand Pa enjoyed his many eggs for breakfast, and lunch, he was growing tired of that irritating rooster squawk. Grand Pa told Grand ma that he did as she requested. He listened and watched.

Grand pa reminded Grandma of the sermon last Sunday at church He said you remember those verses the preacher read from Mark 13:33-37. *Take ye heed, watch and pray for ye know not when the time is.* **34** *For the Son of Man is as a man taking a far journey, who left his house, and gave authority to his servants, and to every man his work, and commanded the porter to watch.***35** *Watch ye therefore: for ye know not when the master of the house cometh, at even, or at midnight, or at the cockcrowing, or in the morning:***36** *Lest coming suddenly he find you sleeping.* **37** *And what I say unto you I say unto all, Watch.*

Grand pa told Grand ma that he believed what the preacher said, and that Jesus would come again. We must always be watchful. For when he returns, there will be judgment and those not under His grace will pay for their sins.

Grand pa went out to the barn. There he found that old loudmouth banty rooster. He said it taxed me, but I told him that soon it will be April 15th. And he better watch and not sleep for the ax man cometh. There will be judgment. The Irritating Rooster Squawk (IRS) would only be an echo from days gone by. Sunday dinner while somewhat small ,was bountiful. No squawk about it.

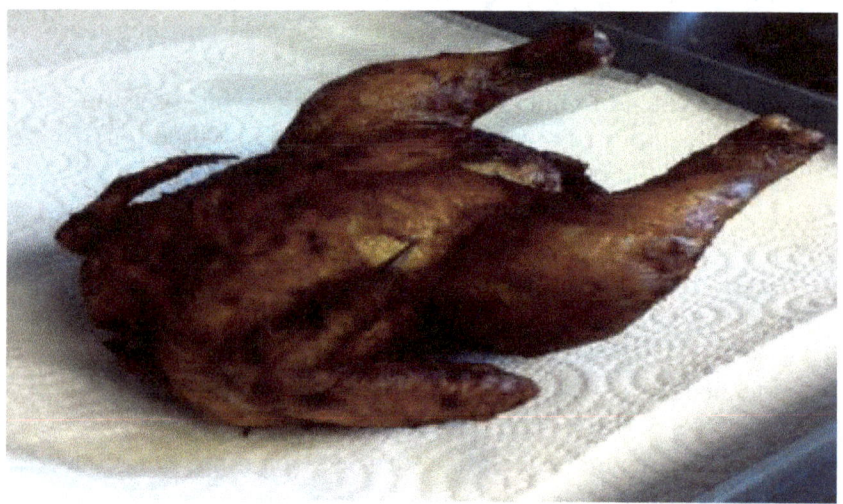

Grandpa- The Doors

Grandpa was standing in front of his old barn's closed double wide doors. He was just standing there. Staring st those doors. I walked up behind him and asked, "What are you looking at?". He replied that there are many a life lesson in doors. There are many way to describe a door. There are physical doors and spiritual doors. The physical doors are Exterior Doors and Interior Doors. Doors of Wooden or Timber, Glass, Steel ,PVC, Fiberglass ,Aluminum Glazed, and Fiber Reinforced Plastic /FRP Doors. There are even boulders and rocks used as doors.

Doors are also classified as to operation: Folding, Sliding ,S winging, Revolving Rolling Shutter, Collapsible and Pivot Doors. They are even identified by the method of construction: Panel, Flush, Louvered and Wire Gauze Doors. Doors are portals where we have ingress into and egress from an enclosure.

The greatest physical door was met by three women who wondered how they would open it. Mark 16 4-8 And when they looked, they saw that the stone was rolled away: for it was very great. And entering the sepulcher, they saw a young man sitting on the right side, clothed in a long white garment; and they were affrighted. And he saith unto them, Be not affrighted: Ye seek Jesus of Nazareth, which was crucified: he is risen; he is not here: behold the place where they laid him. But go your way, tell his disciples and Peter that he goeth before you into Galilee: there shall ye see him, as he said unto you. And they went out quickly and fled from the sepulcher; for they trembled and were amazed: neither said they anything to any *man*; for they were afraid.

The greatest spiritual door is the acceptance of the Lord Jesus Christ as our personal savior. Faith and belief in the birth, death, and resurrection. Being saved, bought by the blood of Jesus shed at the cross. Praying, Confessing and Repenting daily. John 10-7 Then said Jesus unto them again, *Verily, verily, I say unto you, I am the door of the sheep.* John 10:9 *I am the door: by me if any man enter in, he shall be saved, and shall go in and out, and find pasture. John 14-6* Jesus saith unto him, *I am the way, the truth, and the life: no man cometh unto the Father, but by me.*

Psalm 24-7 Lift up your heads, O ye gates; and be ye lift up, ye everlasting doors; and the King of glory shall come in. 8 Who is this King of glory? The LORD strong and mighty, the LORD mighty in battle. 9 Lift up your heads, O ye gates; even lift them up, ye everlasting doors; and the King of glory shall come in. 10 Who is this King of glory? The LORD of hosts, he is the King of glory. Selah.

For those who have accepted Jesus as their personal savior, their door is familiar because they are well acquainted and have an intimate relationship with Him.

For those who have not received Jesus, their life's journey to the door will be hindered by the sin and confusion of the

World.. But if they only believe. then knock on the door.

Mathew 7-7 Ask, and it shall be given you; seek, and ye shall find; knock, and it shall be opened unto you: 8 For everyone that asketh receiveth; and he that seeketh findeth; and to him that knocketh it shall be opened.

Doors usually are gateways or portals from one place to another. One type of door that can be most confusing is the revolving door. Where the occupant is caught in the door and goes in and out repeatedly and never entering. Spiritually it is where we sin and repent, sin again, Accepting not our abominations and accursed things and not doing away with them. Accepting not that you have spoken against Powers and Jesus. 2 Corinthians 2:11 Lest Satan should get an advantage of us: for we are not ignorant of his devices.

Matthew 7:21-23 **21** Not everyone that saith unto me, Lord, Lord, shall enter the kingdom of heaven; but he that doeth the will of my Father which is in heaven. **22** Many will say to me in that day, Lord, Lord, have we not prophesied in thy name? and in thy name have cast out devils? and in thy name done many wonderful works? **23** And then will I profess unto them, I never knew you: depart from me, ye that work iniquity.

James 4:7 Submit yourselves therefore to God. Resist the devil, and he will flee from you.

From your birth you passed through a portal from of your mother's womb into the world. Upon reaching an age of accountability, knowing right from wrong, the Holy Spirit touched the door of your heart. Upon you opening the door and accepting Jesus as your personal savior, you passed into a door of protection and blessings. Daily, praying, repenting, and praising you pressed toward the mark for the prize of the high calling of God in Christ Jesus.

One day you shall stand at a final door. Your mortal body will not pass, but you immortal soul will. The gates of

Heaven. Mathew 26-21 His lord said unto him, Well done, thou good and faithful servant: thou hast been faithful over a few things, I will make thee ruler over many things: enter thou into the joy of thy lord.

Remember the RISEN this Easter. Believe upon Him. Accept Him as your personal savior. Repent, before the outer door shuts. Forever closed. Your immortal soul closed in eternal darkness and sorrow.

REJOICE as He is no longer in the tomb behind a closed stone. PRAISE HIM as He sits on the right hand of the Father in Heaven having defeated Death, Hell, and the Grave.. HE is waiting for your acceptance and home coming. Knock upon His door and it will be opened to you. Enter into eternal light and joy..

Grandpa and the Mule

My grandpa was to say the least a unique man. He had no formal education. He could not read, write, or do math; However, he was considered intelligent among men. His insights were extraordinary. Once I wanted to buy a new car. Of course, I would have to finance it. After looking at several, I told my Grandpa which car I had selected to buy. He said, "wait till Saturday". "I want to show you something before you buy". I waited. I could not think what he could show me. I had completed High school and was in college. What could be possible show me about a new car. I had read everything about them. He could not even read. Then Saturday came. My Grandpa insisted we first visit a used car lot that had several older models of the car I wanted. We walked the lot. Some of those cars really looked bad and drove worst. My Grandpa said" Son, in a few years, after you pay off your car, it will look and drive as these do. See what you will have in 5 years, The new had worn off those for sure. I looked amazed at his wisdom. He then took me to another lot where all their used cars shined and looked great. They even drove better than the first lot. My grandpa said "no man can see the future, but here you can see what your future car will look like when its paid for. I chose a used car..

Ecclesiastes 8- 7 *For he knoweth not that which shall be: for who can tell him when it shall be.*

Mathew 24-36 *But of that day and hour knoweth no man, no, not the angels of heaven, but my Father only.*

The future is unknown. I was so amazed how my Grandpa would know this since he could not read. I asked him how he knew. He smiled and said your Grandma read the Bible to me. He then quoted a scripture Psalm 32-9 *Be ye not as the horse, or as the mule, which have no understanding: whose mouth must be held in with bit and bridle, lest they come near unto thee.*

He said I once bought a young mule. I thought I could train him to work. They are stubborn by nature, but this one would do nothing. He had no understanding of his job on the farm. Even bridled and in front of the plow, he just stood there. However, he was great in pulling a wagon that took your Grandma to Church, but would not move a muscle with the plow. So, your Grandma, a Bible reading woman, said " Psalm 81-12 *So I gave them up unto their own hearts' lust: and they walked in their own counsels.* He said "I did the only thing possible. I choose not to be as the mule, but rather understood the nature of him. I gave this young mule to your Grandma for her Church going and I sought out an older well-trained mule to do the farm work." Without hesitation, the older mule always worked sunup to sundown and never once challenged the gentle tugging of my reins.

The lesson I learned was New is not always better. What appears bright and shiny today, with time, often tarnishes and loses its ability to perform. One cannot see the future. However, if one looks at the past and studies it and trusts it, then one might learn the true value of things and determine if the thing sought after is worthwhile. Proverbs 3-5 **Trust in the LORD with all thine heart; and lean not unto thine own understanding.** *6 In all thy ways acknowledge him, and he shall direct thy paths. 7 Be not wise in thine own eyes: fear the LORD, and depart from evil.*

Romans 15:4 *For whatsoever things were written aforetime were written for our learning, that we through patience and comfort of the scriptures might have hope.*

Titus 1:2 *In* **hope** *of eternal life, which God, that cannot lie, promised before the world began;*

Find an old book, called the Bible. Read it,, Trust it, and you will find your prize, joy, and future.

Grand Pa and the Rats

Grand Pa worked hard all spring and summer. He planted the fields with the help of his old mule. Working from sun to sun, they worked until the time of harvest. He had what they say is a bumper crop in all he planted. .He had put up a lot of different grains, fruits, and vegetables in his old barn. Psalm 67-6 *Then shall the earth yield her increase; and God, even our own God, shall bless us.* This year the old barn was totally full.

Grand Pa was a man who took notice of the seasons and almost all things around him. The direction the wind would blow. The smell of the air. He could tell if it was going to rain or not. The color of the sky and even how the animals were acting. James 3-7 *For every kind of beasts, and of birds, and of serpents, and of things in the sea, is tamed, and hath been tamed of mankind:* The wild animals as well as the barn animals could sense nature and would tell him what was about to happen. When the old cows at the far end of the pasture came running to the cow barn, he knew a storm was coming.

Grand Pa said most animals on the farm have been tamed. But those barn mice and rats were a pest and could not be tamed. He said you would have to pay particular attention to them. He said they eat up your grains and if left unchecked could spread disease. He said they are all around. In the field, in the woods and worst some creep into the barn where the crops are, to steal and devour. He said like your Grandma would say after reading her Bible, Leviticus 11-29 *These also shall be unclean unto you among the creeping things that creep upon the earth, the weasel, and the mouse, and the tortoise after his kind.*

Grandpa said your Grand ma is right about the weasel and the mouse, but I take exception to what your Grandma said. I asked him, how? Why? He replied she speaks of the unclean four-legged critters. I know some rats just down the hollow, the two-legged kind. They often sneak into my barn and try to steal my supplies and harvest. Like the good book says in Psalm 6-30 *Men do not despise a thief, if he steal to satisfy his soul when he is hungry;.* But these rats steal to sell to others, to profit not from their labors, but someone else. Mathew 24- 43 *But know this, that if the goodman of the house had known in what watch the thief would come, he would have watched, and would not have suffered his house to be broken up.* If they truly needed some of my harvest, I would freely give them, You never can tell when the thief will come. You always must be on guard.

I asked him just how he was going to control all those rats to keep them from robbing him and protect his harvest. . He replied, "Did you know there are all kinds of rats. There are brown rats, black rats, white rats and even pack rats. There are almost as many colors of rats as colors of people. Each color thinks it is the most important, but in the end, they are all rats. They are all different, but all the same. No one color of rat matters more than the other, they are all creatures of habit, and each has a degree of intelligence, Some of them think almost human, other think like the fools. Proverbs 14-8 *The wisdom of the prudent is to understand his way: but the folly of fools is deceit.* Some rats play with a trap and eat the cheese, while others are caught in the trap.

Speaking of colors, there is even a snake called the red rat snake." but I knew your Grandma was not one to favor me putting snakes into the barn to control the rats, I got some cats.

I said Grandpa, I know wild feral cats will work on the four-legged rats, but all you got is an old house cat. It would more near play with them than catch and eat them. Then I asked him how you going to control the two-legged kind you spoke about to. He remarked "these will not be ordinary cats. They are special for keeping out the two-legged rats. I was puzzled. I thought to myself, is he going to put a bobcat in the barn?

He said I had to look far and wide to get this cats. I even set some traps in the woods to see if I could catch one. After a few days, I was amazed that I caught two of them. So, I went back to the barn and fixed a nice little area for them to kinda nest in . I built a cage inside so they would not escape. They were frisky little things. So much so, they push over a can of blue paint I had just opened to paint the chicken house side of the barn. Grandma said hens lay better if they see blue and give more eggs. Them crazy wild cats done spilled the paint on their tails. What a site. A blue tailed cat.

Well, it had been just a week after the final harvest when Grand Pa came into the front room and announce that his cat had done caught three mice. He said they are great at the four-legged kind. Now that word is out that my crops are all in, let us see if my special cats can catch the two-legged kind. Job 18-10 *The snare is laid for him in the ground, and a trap for him in the way.*

Must been about 2 am in the morning that cool autumn night, when we heard men yelling and what appeared to be gasping for breath. We all got up and looked outside. Grandma said I think someones in the barn. I see a light out there. She said asked Grandpa if he was going to go out there with his shotgun. He replied do not have to, the cats will do a fine job.

As one of the men ran out of the barn, I heard him say "What kinda critter was that? Black and white body and a blue tail. And what a smell. Let's get out of here. Never saw two men run so fast.

Days later while at the local country store, Grandpa said he was about to but some cooking stuff for Grandma when two men walked in. They reeked of an odor. He asked, "New cologne", and smiled. He now knew who the two-legged thieves were. They had just met his blue tail polecats as we country folks would say. Skunks to city folks.. All the mice had been removed and no longer did he have a threat of two legged rats

Ephesians 4-28 *"Let him that stole steal no more: but rather let him labour, working with his hands the thing, which is good, that he may have to give to him that needeth."*

After a while Grand pa opened the barn doors wide, so the little thief catchers could return to their native surroundings. Legends say that every once in a while you can still see those

little blue tail critters crossing the road. Grand pa was never bothered with barn thieves again.

Grand Pa and the Paint Brush

Grand Pa was a farmer by trade. Being a rural farmer in the early 1920's he had to be self-sufficient. That is, he had to know how to use many tools. Not only know how to use them but fix them when they broke or would not function as they should. One of his most prized tools was a paint brush. He had used it to paint the outside of the house. He painted the inside of the house. All his outbuildings, the chicken coop, the smoke house, the barn and even a few coats of paint on the outhouse. He took extra care in his paint brush as he only had the one. He explained to me, when you have a tool, you must know all its parts. For instance, a paintbrush is made of many parts. The Handle. Every brush has one. The Ferrule, that part of the brush that holds the bristles to the handle. The Bristles, the part of the brush you paint with. The Toe, the very end of the brush. The Belly, the middle of the bristles. The Heel, where the bristles go into the ferrule at the end the handle.

He explained the most important part was the Ferrule. He said most folks never see it for the rest of the brush. It is the part used to strengthen the tool handle, for joining and binding the bristles to the handle.
He said it's kinda like your Grandma's Bible. The binding on

the back holds the Bible's pages together. On the pages are the words written to bind us together in the applying of God's Law and Love.

Psalm 3 says "My son, forget not my law; but let thine heart keep my commandments: For length of days, and long life, and peace, shall they add to thee. Let not mercy and truth forsake thee: **bind** them about thy neck; write them upon the table of thine heart: So shalt thou find favour and good understanding in the sight of God and man."

He said today I am saddening as the ferrule has become uncrimped. It no longer binds. It is the same with the Bible. The world has miss placed and forgotten it binding words. Not only those words that bind us to the Love of Christ, but also our fellow man. Some Churches seems void and unbound, lacking a sense of responsibility. The handle and bristles are disconnected. They function, but are being idle, in their endeavor to worship God and to glorify Him on earth," They offer programs to entertain, but not to develop each individual Christian to attain the full stature of Christ. .

Psalm 119:126" *It is* time for *thee*, LORD, to work: *for* they have made void thy law."

Ezekiel 22:25 There *is* a conspiracy of her prophets in the midst thereof, like a roaring lion ravening the prey; they have devoured souls; they have taken the treasure and precious things; they have made her many widows in the midst thereof. Her priests have violated my law and have profaned mine holy things: they have put no difference between the holy and profane, neither have they shewed *difference* between the unclean and the clean, and have hid their eyes from my sabbaths, and I am profaned among them.

Romans 13:13 Let us walk honestly, as in the day, not in **rioting** and drunkenness, not in chambering and wantonness, not in strife and envying. Let us not violate anything sacred; Let us not treat with abuse, or contempt any person. Let us not **profane** the name of God or the **Scriptures.**

Be of good comfort, be of one mind, live in peace; and the God of love and peace shall be with you. All are equal, coming from the dust and returning to the dust.
1 Thessalonians 5:21 But examine everything carefully; hold fast to that which is good.

Grand Pa laid picked up his paint brush. With a pressing tool he fasten and secured the ferrule. He remarked My ferrule is secure in Jesus, the Christ. My ferrule is tight upon the paintbrush. My brush paints. Does yours?.

Grand Pa-Act Your Age

Grand Pa used to say most people don't know how to act their age. They act plum foolish. They play around being something they were never intended to be. They work at pleasing themselves and being lazy about who they could be. They fiddle about interfering or going off doing something half-cocked without regard to the consequences.

I remember one time when us grand kids were out from the farmhouse after dark. To Grand pa, dark meant time to eat supper and go to bed. So, as we entered the front door, there he stood in his farm overalls and blue-green plaid shirt waiting on us. He said : Where have you been? Do you know what time it is? You are hours late! For supper and bed. I've been waiting for you. I needed to make sure you got home safely. Where were you? We told him that we grand kids were just playing in the cornfield since it had just been harvested. He said : What's the matter with you? You went off half-cocked, not looking or thinking,. I put the old bull out there at night. The cornfield is dangerous at night. That old bull can't see well, and he might charge and trampled you. You kids are old enough to know better than that. Act your age!

After supper and a bath Grandpa set us down to talk to us. We could see he had been truly worried. I remember telling him I was 10 years old and responsible, He said a funny thing , I thought. He remarked you are older than that. I looked puzzled. He said you grand kids know "I 'have not had no schooling. No reading or writing, but I have studied a lot. Mostly animals and of course people. You learn a lot by just watching how folks act."

Grandma read to me in the Bible 1 Corinthians 13:11 *When I was a child, I spake as a child, I understood as a child, I thought as a child: but when I became a man, I put away childish things.*

Grand pa said "Today's it seems a lot of people we think of as adults are still children. Age does not determine the adult status". When a person becomes an adult, it is through a process. It is, not only physical, but emotional and spiritual growth and understanding. Birthdays are not really accurate. He said I never really figured out why we celebrate birthdays. Before we are born, we are conceived. Then after a time we get delivered into the world. Wondered why we never had a conceived day and a delivery day to celebrate our lives? Most of us are about nine months older than out birth date. We were alive inside our mother till the proper time.

He said a child is first created, either male or female. That's all. From that day of delivery, they develop into many kinds of people. A lot depends on environment. That is what they are exposed too during their early years of life. Some follow a straight road, other follow different roads. Some follow roads and they lose their identity. He said no matter which road a baby takes, that child first crawls, then attempts to walk, but always falls. They will keep up this process till they take a first step, then walk. Soon the walk turns into a jog, then a run. Trial and error or learning and recording failures into success. The physical develops from a baby of dependence to a child of independence to a person of strength and physical maturity. Fully developed in stature, but lacking in emotional and spiritual maturity, They can run fast, but they don't know which the right way is to go. Still a child.

The emotional growth stems from all their experiences, expressions, understandings, and regulation of the feelings of joy, sorrow, fear, hate, love, etc. that they have. You kids often would pout, whine, and complain. But as you grew in emotional maturity, you did not let the heat of the mind be prone to anger but stayed in calmness and a state of composure. Proverbs 15:18 *A wrathful man stirreth up strife: but he that is slow to anger appeaseth strife.* Mature emotional adults at any age is when you can respond to situations and control your emotions when dealing with others. Proverbs 15:1-2 1 *A soft answer turneth away wrath: but grievous words stir up anger. 2 The tongue of the wise useth knowledge aright: but the mouth of fools poureth out foolishness.*

An adult would not show a lack of sense; be ill-considered; conduct *a* foolish speech which *was* lacking forethought or caution. Emotional maturity does not let the person rear their reactive head and pout, whine or complain over how they were treated or how things used to be. In doing so, they are still a child. Immature folks that are running down the road, but most often so close to the edge that they are about to crash into my cornfield where that old bull is. He and they won't be happy.

Spiritual growth and understanding is the development of an essential principles of virtues like honesty, genuine love, forgiveness, kindness and speaking the truth . Spiritual Growth is spending time with God,, studying and reading the Bible like your Grandma does. Praying to him – telling him of your questions, worries and concerns like I do.

Separation from God leads to a lack of love for fellow man. It will lead to childish behavior of lying on another character, unkind acts to destroy fellow humans no matter their race, sex, age, or religious affiliation. Still a child.

Today's adult seems to lack wisdom, justice, and judgment, and equity. They may be intelligent, but not wise. They strive for fake news, destructive lies, innuendos to damage the lives and reputation of others. Matthew 24:11 *And many false prophets shall rise and shall deceive many.*

They seek roads away from the main road of life that was given to them. In the Bible, Ecclesiastes 9:11 *I returned, and saw under the sun, that the race is not to the swift, nor the battle to the strong, neither yet bread to the wise, nor yet riches to men of understanding, nor yet favour to men of skill; but time and chance happeneth to them all.*

These are the immature adults that were given time and a chance to grow and understand. These are the adults who did not hear their fathers or forefathers. Proverbs 1-8 *My son, hear the instruction of thy father, and forsake not the law of thy mother.* Proverbs 22- 6 *Train up a child in the way he should go: and when he is old, he will not depart from it.* Putting away childish things and misunderstandings, 1 Corinthians 14-20 *Brethren, be not children in understanding: howbeit in malice be ye children, but in understanding be men.*

Grandpa then turned out the kerosene lamp and said to go to sleep. Before leaving the room, Grand Pa turned and said "Learn to know better. Think with Love, forgiveness and speaking the truth under the direction of Jesus, then you can be a responsible adult and can act your age". Stay out of the cornfield and both you and my old bull will be happy.

Grand pa- The Cluttered Shed

Grandpa was standing just outside his tool shed. Looking into that old rustic room attached to a weathered barn. It was full of his working tools and then some more stuff. Shelves full . Floor full. Not an inch to spare. Grand Pa said "You know this place is like most people lives. Cluttered with vices, regrets, desires, failures, and accomplishments. One cluttered shed!

There were books stacked on one shelf on top of themselves. . There were thirty to forty of them. I found this amazing as Grandpa could not read. So why so many books?, His reply, well even though I cannot read writing, I can read pictures. They give me an ideal of what and how to do my work. He said I keep them to remember how to do things. Proverbs 10:7 *The memory of the just is blessed: but the name of the wicked shall rot.*

Sitting nearby was an old 1930's tube radio that no longer worked. I asked him why did he keep it? He replied that it was to remind him of what he had heard. By listening to old farm radio shows, it provided him with ideals of how to work the fields better. Psalm 1-5 *A wise man will hear, and will increase learning; and a man of understanding shall attain unto wise counsels:*

On a secluded shelf was about twenty-five old empty candy dishes. I had to know why he kept them. He said it was to remind him of the sweet words spoken in his life. Psalms 119:103 *How sweet are thy words unto my taste! Yea, sweeter than honey to my mouth!* The sweetest words heard was from the little church in the cornfield, better than any sweet corn he ever planted or harvested.

Nearby the shelves was an old water bucket. Wood as I remember. It was full, not of water, but of digging tools. Shovels, Hoes. Picks and even a post hole digger. All in one bucket. Then nearby was a full set of canning jars full of nuts, bolts, washers, and screws. Above them on the wall was a full set of hammers arranged by size, small to large. The rest of the shed was full of farming instruments. Rakes, plows, floats, and harnesses for the old mule. What a clutter!

Grandpa said "well then it hit me. 1 Corinthians14/40 *Let all things be done decently and in order.* Well, I had the right intention of storing my tools and supplies. It kinda like most people, they all have a decent plan for life. Then they let fears, rejection or words stop them. Isaiah *32-7 The instruments also of the churl are evil: he deviseth wicked devices to destroy the poor with lying words, even when the needy speaketh right.*

Grand pa's plan was noble. To simply store things when not being used. But his way of storing only led to confusion and clutter. His actions had been direct but meaninglessness to order. So as in life, we place things in a way we think is right, only to find out later that they were confusing and nothing but clutter to our joy and happiness.

Grand pa said, "guess it was now time to unclutter". Ecclesiastes 3:6 *A time to get, and a time to lose; a time to keep, and a time to cast away.*

Luke 12:15 *And he said to them, "Take care, and be on your guard against all covetousness, for one's life does not consist in the abundance of his possessions."* Without God at the center of one's life, life can get confused and cluttered

Grandpa and I spent all day cleaning and rearranging that old shed. Now everything had a place and was in its place. Neat and orderly. Grandpa said **Ephesians** "Neither give place to the devil." 1 Corinthians 14:33 For God is not the author of confusion, but of peace, as in all churches of the saints.

Life's walk is not to be in clutter and confusion. Psalms 37:23 The steps of a good man are ordered by the LORD: and he delighteth in his way.

Is it time to clean out your shed?

Grand Pa and the Book

Job 19-23 *Oh that my words were now written! oh that they were printed in a book! 24 That they were graven with an iron pen and lead in the rock forever!*

A middle-aged man was walking home one Friday .Instead of taking his company bus he decided to walk up the mountain road ,see the beautiful sunset and take a train on the other side. His time calculation went wrong, and it became dark ,he was still on the inclined mountain road .While walking hurriedly he noticed shadow of a man standing near a dim incandescent lamp post .By his standing posture he looked like an old man. He was wearing a baggy cloak seem to have made a century ago. He was holding a book in his hand .The middle-aged man tried to engage in a conversation by asking the time .The old man nodded in a way showing he doesn't know and doesn't care. The man couldn't resist and asked, "what are you holding there". The old man answered, "*It's the last thing a mortal should own*". Amused by this statement the man asked more about the book to which the old man answered, "*the owner of this book becomes rich and gets everything he wants*". The man got interested and asked the old man to sell him that book. The old man said "10,000 dollars" .The man being highly superstitious paid the price and bought the book. As he was leaving down the mountain road the old man stopped him to warn about the book saying, "whatever you do with it ,never open the last page ,or you will die". The man left rather happily despite the warning.

From that day forward the man quit his job , bought a big villa and a sports car on loan and mortgage from his smaller house. He waited for his days to change and started daydreaming about more expensive things thinking the book will show its magic. But that never happened. After being in debt for years he finally lost his patience and decided to look at the last page of the book. He slowly opened the book and saw all pages were empty .He never looked at the pages before as he was only interested in the outcome of owning the book. Fearing for his life he opened the last page and died instantly of cardiac arrest. The last page said "Hard bound ,unruled. $8.99"

Grand pa often said " having a book does not make you wise or rich. But knowing and reading people will. 2 Corinthians 3-18 *Let no man deceive himself. If any man among you seemeth to be wise in this world let him become a fool, that he may be wise.*

Grand pa said there are many kinds of books. The Book about Nature. Just watch the tree, flowers, and the animals. They will tell you about the weather and the time of year. Then there is a Book of Remembrance. History is a good book as it teaches us that life is a branch of knowledge and learning from others. It is recorded in word, song, and stories. It should teach us to grow from past successes and failures. Then as we live there is the greatest book. The Bible which has The Old Testament and The New testament. The rule and guide of our life. After we pass this life ,there are the books of The Record of Every Man's Works and The Lamb's Book of Life.

Grandpa said as there many kinds of books, as there are many different types of people. Each person is a book. Some are beautifully written with many words and accomplishments. . Some are blank pages with no works to describe. Grand pa did not have an extensive library. He only owned one book. But Grandpa did have a vast library of friends. They all were well written and well versed.

What was so amazing was that he carried his only book everywhere he went. He had a small pocket in the front of his bib overalls where he kept it. Why would he carry it if he could not read the book? Then one day while I was watching him as he hooked up the mule to the plow a garden spot. What amazed me was watching him take the book out of his bib, open it and it looked like he was reading something.

But Grandpa could not read. I went closer to see what he was supposedly reading as he was speaking aloud. Then I realized he had opened the book and it was a Bible. He was not reading the book, but rather talking to it. I heard him say, as he open the book, Lord, I hope I have hitched up this old mule straight with the plow so we can make a straight row. Lord I hope I been right enough that you see fit that these crops grow. Lord, if I ain't, please overlook my wrong doings. I will try to do my part and I know you will do yours. Together we can harvest for the family and the church folks. Thank you now Lord. He placed the book back inside his bid. He snapped the bib shut so the book would not fall out. He did not want to lose it. Then with a loud voice he said "Get up mule, "Let's go to work "
.
I remember Grandpa telling us a story of an old devout cowboy who lost his favorite Bible while he was mending fences out on the range. Three weeks later, a mule walked up to him carrying the Bible in its mouth. The cowboy couldn't

believe his eyes. He took the precious book out of the mule's mouth, raised his eyes heavenward and exclaimed, "It's a miracle!" "Not really," said the mule. "Your name is written inside the cover."

Grandpa said, "Now that leaves us to the Book of Life. Will your name be written there? Do you believe in Jesus Christ? His birth, death, and resurrection. And most importantly, His return. Rev 3-5 The one who is victorious will, like them, be dressed in white. I will never blot out the name of that person from the book of life but will acknowledge that name before my Father and his angels.

Grandpa said someday I will get to Heaven. Everything is perfect there. So, I know my eyes will see and I know I will be able to read. Just maybe, I say , just maybe I can look at a page in that book and see your name too. Be Blessed and Believe. Don't leave this life and let your book be blank!

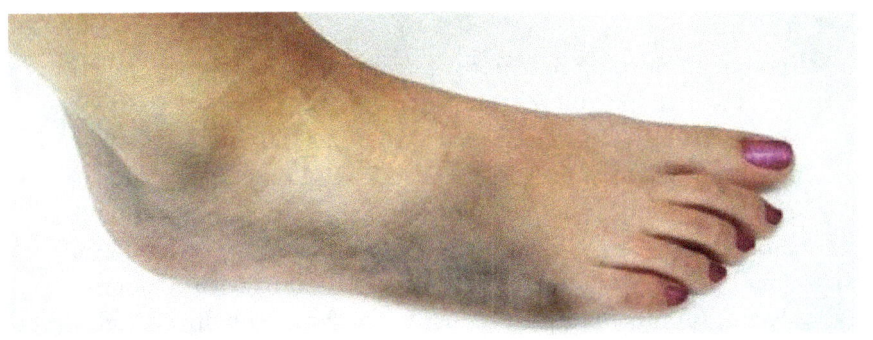

Grand Pa-All Washed Off

Grand pa tells me when him and Grand ma first got married that they were so aware of each other. Both were so considerate. If Grand ma thought Grand pa might be thirsty working in the cornfield, she would bring him water to drink. If Grand Pa thought Grand ma was having trouble with the wood stove, he would bring in the wood and start a fire for her. He said he even helped her cook and he did all the dirty dishes..

It being just one week into their marriage and after a hard day's work both were tired and exhausted. Night had come and they both went to sleep. After a while, Grand ma had to visit the Ladies room. Being so quiet as not to wake her new husband she did not even turn on any lights. Upon attempting to return to the bed, she had forgotten that the foot of the bed had a deacon's bench attached to the foot. At her surprise she walked straight into it, stubbing her toe. The pain was so much she awoke Grand pa. Grand ma cried but refused to go to a doctor. She said it be alright. Grand ma said besides the doctor is eight miles away and it would take us too long to hitch up the mule and wagon to go see him. At this time Grand Pa had no other form of transportation.

The next morning her foot was somewhat swollen. So much so, she had trouble getting into her new black shoes for going to church. Grand ma persisted her foot would be okay and went on to church. Upon returning home she pulled of her shoes with some pain and notice her whole foot was not blue, but black. All over black from the toes to the heel, top and bottom. Grand Pa now insisted she go to a doctor. Again, Grand ma said no, just a hot bath to help her relax and she insisted that it would help reduce the swelling. After being in the tub for maybe ten minutes she led out a scream.

Grand Pa said he ran as fast as he could to help her. When asking her what was wrong, she pointed at her foot. This led to laughter, as Grand ma had washed her foot with a washcloth and amazingly the entire blackness was gone from her foot. Then she remember her new black shoes. Her foot although somewhat swollen had not turned black. Her foot looked almost perfect. The dye of the new shoes had only bled through. Grand ma quipped "from now on if we see a bruise, we will get a wet washcloth to see if it will wash off.

Genesis 18:4 Please let a little water be brought and wash your feet, and rest yourselves under the tree.

Genesis 19-2 And he said, Behold now, my lords, turn in, I pray you, into your servant's house, and tarry all night, and wash your feet, and ye shall rise early, and go on your ways

Ezekiel 36:25 Then will I sprinkle clean water upon you, and ye shall be clean: from all your filthiness, and from all your idols, will I cleanse you. 26 A new heart also will I give you, and a new spirit will I put within you: and I will take away the stony heart out of your flesh, and I will give you a heart of flesh. 27 And I will put my spirit within you, and cause you to walk in my statutes, and ye shall keep my judgments, and do them. 28 And ye shall dwell in the land that I gave to your fathers; and ye shall be my people, and I will be your God.

Jeremiah 33:8 I will cleanse them from all their iniquity by which they have sinned against Me, and I will pardon all their iniquities by which they have sinned against Me and by which they have transgressed against Me.

1 John 1-7 But if we walk in the light, as he is in the light, we have fellowship one with another, and the blood of Jesus Christ his Son cleanseth us from all sin. 9 If we confess our sins, he is faithful and just to forgive us our sins, and to cleanse us from all unrighteousness.

Water may have washed away a dyed-on bruise. But only the blood Of Jesus can cleanse the soul of all its sins and Iniquities. What can wash away my sin? Nothing but the blood of Jesus.

What can make me whole again? Nothing but the blood of Jesus.

Grand Pa -The Quilt

I remember my grandmother making a patchwork quilt. She would use our old work clothes and towels. Sometimes an ocassional worn out Sunday dress outfit. She would cut them into pieces. She saved only the best for the quilt. The worst were disgarded as rags.

Those best remnents removed from the tattered clothing, placed into amazing designs and patterns. Sewn together with warmth, love and joy. The worst always set aside. Used to clean up the dirt, spoils and spills. Then disgarded as trash. Just filthy rags. No soap , she said. No detergent could clean those rags. They were left to be burned in the fire pit and the ashes blown into the wind.

I am reminded that life is kinda like a grandmothers quilt..The best pieces kept in our memories. Those in which our lives which are filled with love family, joy and God. Those pieces that give us wisdom,. Patterns created that are gracious ,patient, tolerent and understanding.

Then there are life's rags.The fabric of our life, times and events sewn together which are at covered in the sins of man, The fifthy rags. The pieces that were once whole and new now full of holes, ragged and empty destroyed by our sins of lust, greed, and envy. The unclean soiled past that harbors the undesirables of guilt, shame and, in many cases, the acute awareness of spiritual uncleanliness.

1 John 1-8 *If we say that we have no sin, we deceive ourselves, and the truth is not in us. 9 If we confess our sins, he is faithful and just to forgive us our sins, and to cleanse us from all unrighteousness.*

Isaiah 64:6 *"But we are all as an unclean thing, and all our righteousnesses are as filthy rags; and we all do fade as a leaf; and our iniquities, like the wind, have taken us away."*

History tell us that a quilt was also once called a *gambeson* . The gambeson was used both as a complete armour unto itself and underneath a cushion to the body that would chafing. It was very insulatory and thus uncomfortable, but its protection was vital for the soldier.

As a soldier in the Army of the Lord, we too must put on a quilt(armor). The full armor of God. Ephesians 6:13-17: "Therefore put on the full armor of God, so that when the day of evil comes, you may be able to stand your ground, and after you have done everything, to stand. Stand firm then, with the belt of truth buckled around your waist, with the breastplate of righteousness in place, and with your feet fitted with the readiness that comes from the gospel of peace. In addition to all this, take up the shield of faith, with which you can extinguish all the flaming arrows of the evil one. Take the helmet of salvation and the sword of the Spirit, which is the word of God."

I remember my grandma's quilt of remnants. It was made with three sailing ships designed into it on every row . She told me that they were to remind me that no matter what row of life I may be on or even where life may take me, that there was always a first ship ahead of me to pull me through. My second ship whose destiny I controlled. A third ship behind me to remind me that I too must assist others. She had names for the ships.

The first ship, FAITH. Hebrews 11:1 *Now faith is the substance of things hoped for, the evidence of things not seen.* She told me to always believe in God and His promises. Then no matter the storm, no matter the tempest, there would always be a blessing ahead for me. It may not come when you want, or be the blessing you desire, but it will always be the one you need.

The second ship she named LOVE .John 3-16 *For God so loved the world, that he gave his only begotten Son, that whosoever believeth in him should not perish, but have everlasting life.* She told me that in life there would be a time that you must give of myself to others. A time to feel the needs of others and offer emotional support to their woes. Comfort them in distress.

The third ship following mine was named CHARITY. 1 Corinthians 13:2 **2** *And though I have the gift of prophecy, and understand all mysteries, and all knowledge; and though I have all faith, so that I could remove mountains, and have not charity, I am nothing.* She said give and it will be given back many times over. It does not have to be money or material things, but time spent with another as a helping hand. She said give and it will be given unto you.

Grandpa said that Grandma made some of the best quilts. They were created with a bible message and offered to the grand kids as a covering of warmth, love, and protection. Her quilts were a profession of what she believed. Her belief in the full armor of God. His truth and righteousness. The gospel of faith, love, salvation, the Word of God, and prayer. They are the tools God has given us, through praise to Him that we can be spiritually victorious, overcoming Satan's attacks and temptations.

Grandpa said even though the quilts when new were fresh and clean, that after a time when they became worn, that they were even better. Full of holes, how could that be? Then I read from an unknown author:

As I faced my Maker at the last judgment, I knelt before the Lord along with all the other souls.

Before each of us, our lives were laid out, like the cloth squares of a quilt, in many piles. An angel sat before each of us sewing our quilt squares together into a tapestry that represented our entire life.

As my angel took each piece of cloth off the pile, I noticed how ragged and empty each of my squares looked. They were filled with giant holes. Each square was labeled with a part of my life that had been difficult; the challenges and temptations I had faced in life every day. The hardships I had endured were the largest holes of all.

I glanced around me. Nobody else had such squares. Other than a tiny hole here and there, the other tapestries were filled with rich color, the bright hues of worldly fortune. I gazed upon my own life and was disheartened.

Like binding air, my angel sewed together the ragged pieces of cloth that seemed threadbare and empty.

The time came when each life had to be displayed and held up to the light--the scrutiny of truth. The others rose, each person holding up their own tapestries; so, filled their lives had been. My angel looked up and nodded for me to rise.

My gaze dropped to the ground in shame. I hadn't possessed all the earthly fortunes. I had possessed love and laughter in my life, but there had also been trials of illness, wealth, and false accusations that took from me my world. I had needed to start over many times. I had often struggled with the temptation to quit, only to muster the strength to pick up and begin again. I had also spent many nights on my knees in prayer, asking for help and guidance in my life. I had often endured ridicule. But each time I had offered my pain up to the Father in hopes that I would not melt beneath the judgmental gaze of other people.

But now I had to face the truth. My life was what it was, and I had to accept it for what it was.

I rose and slowly lifted the combined squares of my life to the light.

An awe-filled gasp filled the air. I gazed around at the others who stared at me with wide eyes.

Then, I looked upon the tapestry before me. Light flooded the many holes, creating an image: the face of Christ.

Then the Lord stood before me, with warmth and love in His eyes. He said, "Every time you gave over your life to Me, it became My life, My hardships, and My struggles. Each point of light in your life represents each time you stepped aside and let Me shine through until there was more of Me than there was of you."

May all our quilts be threadbare and worn, allowing Christ to shine through!

I still have that old sailing ship quilt. Yes it has a few holes, but when I investigate them, I see Grand ma love for me, and I see Jesus Christ shining through her.

Grand Pa , Baseball, and Dad

Grand Pa was not very adept at playing sports. He walked with a limp. He said it happen as he fell out of the hay barn onto the ground. He did not land right. He said as he grew up, there was no time for sports, just work. The only thing he was adapt at was playing a Juice harp. Now he could play some music. Psalm 33-3 *Sing unto him a new song; play skillfully with a loud noise.* He would place that instrument between his teeth and move his mouth and make different sounds.

Several years went by and at the age of twelve, I played Little League Baseball. It was a fun time. I made the team and played Third base. Grand Pa was made proud. Grandpa had retired from farming, and he learned the game of baseball. He said he enjoyed watching us kids run around the ball field. It was a lot better place for us than trampling down his cornfield.

During one on my games, the Umpire that was to call the balls and strikes was not able to make the game. The visiting team suggested that of all people to be behind the plate and to call those balls and strikes was my father. One of Grand pa sons-in-law. Grand pa took his usual seat in the stands. Well not really stands, just a few old planks nailed to a fallen tree near the ball field. Grand pa said he liked to sit in that special spot as it was near a shade tree right behind home plate. He also said he would not yell at the umpire when the call was wrong. But he would sure play him a tune on his juice harp if it was.. Loud plops and twangs. It was heard often.

That day, the games progressed well till my time to bat. The first pitch was over my head and what did I hear "STRIKE ONE'! With a confused glanced I looked at my father. Then came the second pitch which was so far outside the plate, I believe it was in another zip code. Again, what did I hear "STRIKE TWO! This time I had a definite stare at my father. For the first time I heard Grand pa yelling from the stands. "PUT YOUR GLASSES ON"! Several loud juice harp twangs were heard. Well, here it came, the final pitch to me. Not high, not outside, but it literally rolled across the plate. It hit the dirt about two feet in front of home plate and rolled across. You guessed it. In a loud distinct voice, my dad said, "STRIKE THREE"! I just laid my bat down. I said nothing.

Since I made the third out, I walked to my third base position and played the rest of the game. After the game, I heard my Grandpa question my Dad about his calls to me while the rest of his calls were so fair. He spoke in words that I would never forget. He said," I showed no favoritism toward him, rather adversity, and he stood after each call and chose to continue without words or giving up". He played with character. Instead of taking it as a defeat, he rather choose to encourage his team. To play on. I think that's why they won. As he walked away, his last words was "I did it, cause you see "That's, my boy".

Grand pa looked at him and said he understood. He remarked that It took courage on his part to teach me during my game. Dad replied , well in his life there will be many trials. They will not be easy, and he will have to act with faith and courage. "Never give up or in". Proverbs 3-5-6 T*rust in the LORD with all thine heart; and lean not unto thine own understanding. 6 In all thy ways acknowledge him, and he shall direct thy paths.*

Grand pa later remarked to my Dad, while you are my son-in-law, your raising your son in the proper way. Proverbs 22-6 *Train up a child in the way he should go: and when he is old, he will not depart from it* , I am proud to call you "Son" Grand pa got to see many more baseball games. His playing of the juice harp at games became almost a necessity.. Years passed and Grand pa loud juice harp playing was no more. He had played his last song :"What a friend we have in Jesus". He was now playing with a heavenly choir.

Many more years later, as my Dad was in a nursing home for physical therapy, approaching his 95th birthday. My wife and I visited him often. He would often recall that baseball game and remind me to trust Jesus. His memory would sometimes fade. On this one occasion when my wife and I visited him., I will never forget. My wife approached him .My Dad looked at her and asked her "Do I know you?" You look familiar, but I can't place you". This made my wife very sad as they had known each other for many, many years. As I had parked the car and she had gone in first, she was in his room trying to prepare herself to tell me that Dad might not remember me. As I walked down a long corridor to his room, my wife remarked "Do you know who that is coming there" My dad in a strong voice filled with joy simply said "*That's, my Boy*"! He had not ,nor did he ever forget me.

Shortly thereafter both Dad and Grand pa were united. The winter leagues were playing. I am sure Grand pa was playing his juice harp and Dad singing .On the way home from Dad's funeral, playing on the radio was an old familiar song ""Take me out to the ball game". It brought back memories of long ago. Shortly, after arriving back home , I picked up my Bible. I began to read.

Mark 1-9 *And it came to pass in those days, that Jesus came from Nazareth of Galilee, and was baptized of John in Jordan. 10 And straightway coming up out of the water, he saw the heavens opened, and the Spirit like a dove descending upon him: 11 And there came a voice from heaven, saying, Thou art my beloved Son, in whom I am well pleased.* In other words , "**That's, my Boy**"

2 Peter 1-16 *For we have not followed cunningly devised fables, when we made known unto you the power and coming of our Lord Jesus Christ but were eyewitnesses of his majesty. 17 For he received from God the Father honor and glory, when there came such a voice to him from the excellent glory, This is my beloved Son, in whom I am well pleased.* **"That's, my Boy**"!

John 17-1 *When Jesus had spoken these words, he lifted up his eyes to heaven, and said, "Father, the hour has come; glorify your Son that the Son may glorify you, 2 since you have given him authority over all flesh, to give eternal life to all whom you have given him. 3 And this is eternal life, that they know you, the only true God, and Jesus Christ whom you have sent. 4 I glorified you on earth, having accomplished the work that you gave me to do. 5 And now, Father, glorify me in your own presence with the glory that I had with you before the world existed.*

My earthly Grand pa and my Dad had passed on to eternity.

My heavenly Father, sits on his throne in *indescribable* Glory and Majesty, My earthly Dad gave me his greatest gift as he was near his final days when he proudly said, **"That's my Boy!"** Philippians 3:14 *I press toward the mark for the prize of the high calling of God in Christ Jesus. Through adversity, troubles, and trials, I strive to keep a moral character, encouraging others, proclaiming Christ, knowing the Victory is mine.* My greatest desire is to hear my Father in Heaven proclaim proudly and boldly "**That's, my Boy**" " Well *done*, good and faithful servant; you have been faithful over a few things, I will make you ruler over many things. Enter into the joy of your lord.'

Grand Pa and the Gift

Grand Pa thought even with some farming setbacks, it still had been a wonderful year. This year it seemed that the crows found a friend in his old man scarecrow. He with his blue coveralls and bright red flannel shirt filled with hay, standing proudly in the corn field. . Truly, was a scary site to us grand kids, but not to those crows. Grandpa even tried going into the corn field himself and stand there like the scare crow to scare off those pesky birds. Nothing seem to work, That is till one day when Grand ma and her broom came racing into the field and scared off them birds. Grand pa knew then how to keep those birds off his crops. He got an old dress from grand ma, and old bonnet. He filled them with straw to fill them out. Then he went and got one of grand ma old brooms and placed it, so it looked like she was waving it. That did it, no more crows, and a great crop. All thanks to grandma, well kinda.

Thanksgiving day had just passed and now it was time for Grand ma to do her Christmas shopping. She had only a sparse budget, so her choices of gifts were limited. Grand pa said she would save all year for this special time of giving to family and friends.

Now for the Grand kids, we all knew what we were going to receive. A crisp new one-dollar bill and our favorite bar of candy. We had gotten the same gifts every Christmas since we were born. The candy came as Grand ma ran a candy store out of her house. Once a month a traveling salesman would come by and sell Grand ma his candy wholesale. She in turn would sell as they say retail. She sold it for whatever she thought the local kids could afford. I once saw her sell a dime piece of candy for a penny. Neighbors around were just plain poor folks. No kids ever came for candy that they did not get some. Even if the payment was going to the well and get her a bucket of water. She said she only sold the candy to help Grand pa have money to operate the farm. She often would say, Kids, you see that corn field, that's real candy's corn there. Her money bought the seeds.

Of course, us grand kids would raid her supply of candy. Each looking for their favorite. No matter how much candy Grand ma might sell, there was always a bar of our favorite candy hidden back for that special grandchild. Our special gift on each visit. The most amazing thing was that out of seven grand kids, not any two wanted the same candy. Or if we did, grand ma always save back the right number of candy bars for us.

Grand pa would by now have sold off his selling crops and Grand ma would have canned up the eating crops. Grand pa would always set aside a portion especially for Grand ma and her Christmas shopping. Some years she would have plenty and others not so much. This year was a not so much year. She told Grand pa, I got everyone a gift except for your cousin J.R. Grandma quizzed Grandpa; you know I never have known what his real name is. All I ever heard was J.R. Grandpa said well he was named after his daddy. Grandma said well should he not be a junior, not J,R,. Grand pa said nah. His daddy's name is Jordan River Sweet, So everyone knew that name was taken, so they call his son J.R Sweet. as not to confuse them.

Now cousin J.R. was not an ordinary person. His name was J.R, as Grand pa said. He also said he should have been called P.L. It stood for Plum Lazy. J.R.. was as they say tighter than bark on a log. He never bought any Christmas presents, but always had a gift. You see folks around here believed he invented the re-gift idea. He also told Grand pa that he was not lazy, just good at doing nothing. Since he did not finish doing nothing yesterday, he had to do it more today.

Time drew nearer to when cousin J.R. and his family would come to Grand Pa to exchange Christmas gifts. Grand ma grew worried as she had nothing for cousin J.R. The came Grand pa to the rescue as he remember two Christmas past that cousin J.R.. had given him a pair of stripped toe, purple-orange gopher pictured argyle socks that he refused to wear.. Grand pa said let's give them back to him. I still have them in the cedar chest wrapped in the same wrapping that he gave to me two years ago. Grand ma did not like the idea, but she went along. Grand ma said I don't have any extra candy to give him, but I will put a dollar in each sock.

Time past and it was Christmas time again. I knew my Christmas candy and dollar would be waiting. All the family was gathered, including cousin J.R... This year cousin J.R.. smiled big and told Grand pa that he had travel many miles just to get him his present. Grand pa was somewhat excited to see what cousin J.R. had to give. As Cousin J.R.. handed Grand pa his present, Grand pa kinda said "huh" under his breath. Grand ma said, "Open your gift". Grand pa was no psychic, but he knew what was in the package. Grand pa said I will open it later Christmas Day. You guess it, those stripped toe, purple-orange gopher pictured argyle socks given back to him. Grand pa just smiled and said Thankyou, Merry Christmas". Grand pa then just went to the back room, opened the old cedar chest he had and placed the package back inside. No one the wiser.

Twenty- six years past and for thirteen of those years Grand pa got stripped toe, purple-orange gopher pictured argyle socks. They kept floating back and forth from J.R.to Grand Pa to J.R.. It seemed like neither one of those two men ever liked stripped toe, purple-orange gopher pictured argyle socks.. It truly was the gift that no one wanted.

A couple of years passed, and again Grand ma felt a little short of Christmas money. I am being in the middle of the seven grandkids was asked if instead of my usual Christmas gift that I get something different. The older grandkids needed money for school things and the younger grand kids need something from Santa. I said it would be okay with me. On that cold winter Christmas day, I received the best gift ever. Grand pa and Grand ma went to grand pa cedar chest and gave me a package. Grand ma said she hoped I liked them and was sorry it was not more. With excitement I open the gift. There they were. A pair of stripped toe, purpleorange gopher pictured argyle socks. I politely said thank you and Merry Christmas. Then as I was about to roll them up and place them inside my winter coat's pocket, I felt something. Inside each sock was a dollar bill. This year instead of one dollar, I got two. What a Christmas blessing.. Grand pa and Grand ma both laughed. Grand pa said I told you cousin P.L. was lazy. He never even opened the present or looked inside. He is still doing nothing but complaining about his cold feet.

Psalm 10-4,5 **4** He becometh poor that dealeth with a slack hand: but the hand of the diligent maketh rich.**5** He that gathereth in summer is a wise son: but he that sleepeth in harvest is a son that causeth shame.

Psalm 13-4 **T**he soul of the sluggard desireth, and hath nothing: but the soul of the diligent shall be made fat.

Acts 2-38 Then Peter said unto them, Repent, and be baptized every one of you in the name of Jesus Christ for the remission of sins, and ye shall receive the gift of the Holy Ghost.

James 1-17 Every good gift and every perfect gift is from above, and cometh down from the Father of lights, with whom is no variableness, neither shadow of turning

Grand pa smiled and was glad that I was happy. He said even the worst gift can be the best gift.

Grand Pa and the Angels

I remember one hot summer day when Grandpa was resting under a small grove of gray pine trees. I heard Grandma hollered at him to watch out for us grand kids. Her little angels. His head bent, hat over his eyes with a gentle snore, he watched us. Not sure if he knew, but as he slept, we watched him too. 1 Thessalonians 5-6. *Therefore, let us not sleep, as do others; but let us watch and be sober.*

It became a game. The watched being the watchers. All was going well till one of the grand kids did something that they were not supposed to do. It was like he could see even with his eyes closed. He would open his eyes, raise his head, push back his hat and then no more snoring, but a firm voice we would hear " I saw what you did". Daniel 4:13 *I saw in the visions of my head upon my bed, and behold, a watcher and a holy one came down from heaven;* Hebrews 4-13 *Nothing in all creation is hidden from God's sight. Everything is uncovered and laid bare before the eyes of him to whom we must give account.*

Now a few summers passed, and Grand pa was told he would have to have gall bladder surgery. Before going into surgery, the doctor told him he had found quite a large mass near the gall bladder. He wanted to go in and survey the area and determine even if Grandpa should even have the surgery. The doctor said it could be bad. At first, Grandpa was a bit concerned. Then he remember that his Father in Heaven watches over him. So, Grandpa went under the watchful care of an Anesthesiologist and the Surgeon. All went well, the mass about the size of a coffee cup was some scar tissue from a previous surgery, Nothing serious. The doctor removed the mass and the gall bladder.

Released from the hospital, Grandpa returned home. Now at this time Grandpa had moved into the twentieth century. He had bought a used black and white television. He said he got it to watch the weather, as his senses had dulled and except for his arthritis he could not tell the weather.

Grand ma fixed him a nice hot lunch and made his favorite chair as comfortable as she could so he could recover from the surgery. Grand pa started watching a TV show. A woman on the program said God had told her to go to a cemetery and take pictures of Spirits and Angels. They showed some pictures, but all Grand pa saw was blurred lights. She said the bright hovering Angels were those who had just recently acquired a new soul from the recently departed..

Grand ma told him she would go sleep in the front room so not to disturb him in his sleep. She said she did not want to bump into him and cause him any pain. That night Grand pa tried to sleep. He had a sudden pain. His eyes opened and he saw on the right side of the foot of his bed a light hovering above. He thought, about that TV show, Angels here! He thought he must be dreaming. His eyes still half shut, he thought No, I am not dreaming. So, he again opened his eyes. By now the shimmering light was slowing moving to the left side of the bed. Again, he just knew he was dreaming, so he pinched himself to be sure. The pain from the pinch assured him that he was indeed awake. This time the hovering light was moving towards the headboard and directly toward him. All this time that light was hovering, watching, and coming closer to him.

In a half dazed , half-awake state of mind, the realization struck him that an Angel was coming after him to meet Jesus. So, he thought, since I am awake, I will turn on my night light and meet my Angel face to face.
And if they have come to get someone, I will tell them Grand ma asleep in the front room, Go see her.

To his surprise, it was only a Mylar balloon coming towards him. It had come loose from a potted plant someone had given his as a recovery present. Floating loosely under the movement of air from the ceiling fan, it was wandering about the room. But he said to himself, Wait, I saw a light.

Turning off his night light, he looked about his bedroom, There at the window, a light., He then saw a streetlight that had been installed by the electric company where one was not before. This had been done while he was in the hospital. The light had been shining thru his bedroom widow and bouncing off the balloon as it floated around him. He had been watched!

As he laid back down to sleep, the awareness came to him that Angels truly had been all around him. During his surgery and recovery with the Doctors, Nurses, Hospital Staff, and his wife, all who watched over him and heard his voice as he required healing. Psalm 34-7 *The angel of the LORD encampeth round about them that fear him, and delivereth them.* Psalm 34-15 *The eyes of the LORD are upon the righteous, and his ears are open unto their cry.* Hebrews 13-2 *Be not forgetful to entertain strangers: for thereby some have entertained angels unawares.* Psalm 91-11 *For he shall give his angels charge over thee, to keep thee in all thy ways.*

We may not be aware, but Angels are with us, some seen, most unseen. Always watching, reporting, and keeping us in all our ways.

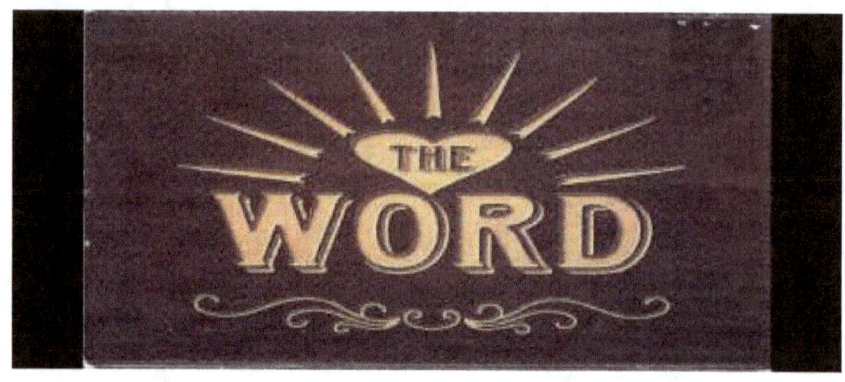

Grandpa-Words

It was a wet spring day. Rain had been falling for over a week. The ground was soaked. The cornfield needed to be plowed, but it would only leave a muddy mess if it was. Dreary and wet day. Gray skies and low clouds. On the front porch sat Grand Pa. I asked him what he was doing? He was silent. Then he said, I am just listening to the sound of the rain. It is speaking to me. I looked puzzled. I said I hear the rain beating down on the old tin roof on the front porch. But it's not speaking to me. I don't hear any words.

Grandpa said to drag up a chair. He swayed back and forth on the old country swing. He had something to tell me. He said I hear words everywhere. You do know that words are simply sounds. Sometimes they are understood by the ear. Sometimes it's the eye that see them as writings or pictures. Some sounds are just an utterance. Some words may be giving a direction to follow. Other words are an assurance or a promise. But no matter the method of knowing the words, they are all a signal. Some show intelligence, others show ignorance. Some are to help, others to hurt.

The greatest word I ever hear was from the old preacher who came to our cornfield church. It was from the bible.

John **1** *In the beginning was the Word, and the Word was with God, and the Word was God.* **2** *The same was in the beginning with God.* **3** *All things were made by him; and without him was not anything made that was made.* **4** *In him was life; and the life was the light of men.* **5** *And the light shineth in darkness; and the darkness comprehended it not.*

Grandpa told me that this meant that there was an assurance, a direction, and a promise from God. If we listen with our hearts, then we can hear and understand. God made all things, even the rain. Even now, look, the rain is only a mist, a light sprinkle. The clouds are thinning. I hear God telling me that the rain will soon be over. The worst part has past. Now with the passing rain comes the light that he has made and given to me, See the rainbow-the promise. The life of the seeds in my farm field will grow. Their harvest will bring life to me and my family with food. The crushed grape seeds would give us canola oil to light our lamps . We will give words of praise and thanksgiving to Him. We can even feed those without. Those who are in darkness and don't understand how to listen to God's word. We can feed them with food for their body and words for their soul..

Grandpa said as you go through life, many words and sounds will come at you. Starting at your birth, all babies are listening closely to the words and sounds all around them. They will begin to sort out their meanings Some are to educate. Some are to encourage. Sometimes when words are spoken with love, they are even for correction. Corinthians 13:11 *When I was a child, I spake as a child, I understood as a child, I thought as a child: but when I became a man, I put away childish things.*

Grandpa then warned, even as a child we must be careful of the words we could hear. Cruel people will say cruel words in front of their children. Then the cycle continues until the child thinks that this is normal. Ephesians 5-6 *Let no man deceive you with vain words: for because of these things cometh the wrath of God upon the children of disobedience.*

Often people with an agenda contrary to God's will for His people will use words of propaganda to distort the Truth. It is true, misery does love company. 1 Corinthians 15-33 **Be not deceived: evil communications corrupt good manners. 34** *Awake to righteousness, and sin not; for some have not the knowledge of God: I speak this to your shame.*

Grandpa said that for those who use words of deception and bias. they will not go unpunished. They may bend the law of man, but God is the final judge. Matthew 12- 6 *But I say unto you, That every idle word that men shall speak, they shall give account thereof in the day of judgment.*

Grandpa said if we can't say something good about someone we should keep quiet. Proverbs 10-19 *In the multitude of words there wanteth not sin: but he that refraineth his lips is wise.*

Grandpa said, now I am in my aged years, I have weathered the storms and rain of life. I have heard and seen good things and bad. Sometimes the words were spoken in a language I did not understand, But if they were spoken with a smile, I knew they were friendly and were to help me understand Since I went to the church service at the church in the cornfield and I meet Jesus, I try to speak with a smile and with brotherly love. My life's purpose is to farm. Toil the ground. Turning it from a hard place to a soft place where a harvest can be planted and grown. Turning a hard heart to a soft heart. To let all men, know about Him and help them out of their ignorance and darkness and grow into the Light..

The rain stopped. Grandpa and I just sit and listen, The birds were now talking to us.

Grandpa-The Snakes and the Birds

Grandpa farm was several acres. A lot of it was in pastures for his farm animals. Beyond the pastures laid the cornfield. Majestically rising above the farm was a ridge line full of woods. Trees of all sorts. Pine trees, Oak trees. Maple trees. Cedar trees. Under them laid a layer of underbrush that in some places even a rabbit could not get through.

The trees were all heights. In the trees were nests of all kinds of birds and squirrels. Under the trees nearest the cornfield on the southeast corner laid an outcropping of rocks. Grandpa said for us to be extra careful there. I asked him why?

He said <u>Proverbs 30:19</u> The way of an eagle in the air; the way of a serpent upon a rock; the way of a ship in the midst of the sea; and the way of a man with a maid.

Down upon the rocks on a sunny day, you will find snakes warming themselves . He said, "you know there are two kinds of snakes down there" There are those that make noise (rattlesnakes) and those that don't (copperheads.) One will let you know not to come close, the other only lets you know after it bites you.

When you are near the rocks, be extra quiet. No talking. Ecclesiastes 10:11 *Surely the serpent will bite without enchantment; and a babbler is no better.* If you are near the rocks and just babbling, you won't hear the noisy ones. Be careful. Be quit and if you hear a noise, be still. See where it comes from and then choose wisely a way to go.

He said if you are moving about, you are like digging a ditch with your feet or at least breaking the ground. He said don't trample the grass on the rocks, for if you do, you will get bitten, Ecclesiastes 10:8 *He that diggeth a pit shall fall into it; and whoso breaketh an hedge, a serpent shall bite him.*

He followed by saying before you get to the outcropping of rocks, look to the trees. Looks for the birds. If there are in there nest and singing, there will be no snakes. But if you see them darting downward and squawking, toward the rocks, they are fighting off a snake. It may be a silent snake, so they are letting you know danger is near. Genesis 3:14 *And the LORD God said unto the serpent, Because thou hast done this, thou art cursed above all cattle, and above every beast of the field; upon thy belly shalt thou go, and dust shalt thou eat all the days of thy life:* That will be the time to back away and find a new direction.

Grandpa said that life was a lot like those woods and rocks. There would be times when obstacles like the underbrush would seem impassable to get through. Things like sickness disease, death, loss of job, loss of marriage and loss of friends.

Then there would be times of love and joy. Just as there would be joy when the birds would be singing in the treetops. There would also be danger on the rocks as in the snakes. Danger as in sin. Romans 3:23 *For all have sinned and come short of the glory of God;* Sin that sometime makes a noise and other times is so silent, it destroys us before we even know it.

Grandpa said, but if we know Jesus as our personal Savior, and we have accepted Him as our Lord and Protector, He will defeat the serpent and we shall be with Jesus for eternity. Revelations 12-9 *And the great dragon was cast out, that old serpent, called the Devil, and Satan, which deceiveth the whole world: he was cast out into the earth, and his angels were cast out with him.*
10And I heard a loud voice saying in heaven, Now is come salvation, and strength, and the kingdom of our God, and the power of his Christ: for the accuser of our brethren is cast down, which accused them before our God day and night.11And they overcame him by the blood of the Lamb, and by the word of their testimony; and they loved not their lives unto the death.

Grandpa said you kids know that snakes are like thieves John 10:10 *The thief cometh not, but for to steal, and to kill, and to destroy: I am come that they might have life, and that they might have it more abundantly.*

Grandpa said you know God loves you and wants to protect you. Just believe and accept. John 3-16 *For God so loved the world, that he gave his only begotten Son, that whosoever believeth in him should not perish, but have everlasting life.*
 The snakes of your life will then be cast out and destroyed. Your birds will then sing and praise.

Grand Pa- The Farewell

It was rather a warm summer day. The sun was shining so bright. Not a cloud in the sky. Just blue skies. A soft summer breeze blowing . The wind was winding its way around Grand pa's old corn field. I had wandered into the harvested field looking for Grand Pa. The field was desolate. Just remnants of a harvested corn field. A few old corn stalks. No Grandpa.

I ran back to the house to see if he was there. I went in the old farmhouse by the back porch. I walked past the watering bucket with its shinning dipper that everyone shared to get a drink of water. The back wall of the porch held a broken mirror that Grandpa used to do his morning shave. Next to the mirror was a shelf where the wash pan sat that we all used to wash our hands at eating time. But No Grandpa.

I went on into the house where the first room I entered was the kitchen, The old wood stove had a fire going and was sitting ready to have Grand ma cook on it. The old wooden pantry with a broken door held all the pots and pans that Grand ma used. One large iron skillet's handle hung hooked on a nail driven into one side of the pantry. The smell of last night's cornbread still resonated from it. But no Grandpa.

Searching the rest of the old farmhouse was easy. It had a front room with a long front porch and then a bedroom.. To imagine that at one time Grand pa and Grand ma and five kids lived in this one-bedroom house. The bathroom was the old fashion kind- outside. It was not the most modern of bathrooms, but in the neighborhood where it was first constructed, the locals thought it extraordinary as it was a two seated with a wall dividing the seats so two people could use at the same time if necessary.

I searched both inside the house and knocked upon the outhouse door, but no Grandpa. Where could he be?. I thought only place left was the barn, So there I ran. I went into the front door. I looked at his storage shed full of tools and well junk. I looked at the side where the laying chicken were resting. I heard them clucking and knew they were doing their business. Eggs for breakfast tomorrow. I climbed up the hay loft and looked everywhere. But still no Grandpa.

Then I climbed upon the bales of hay till I reached the top barn doors in the hay loft. I opened them wide. Up here I could see almost a mile in any direction. I looked north toward the house and pond. No Grandpa. I looked south toward the cornfield, No Grandpa. I looked toward the upper ridge line and the outcropping of rocks where the snakes sunned. But no Grandpa.

I finally looked toward the west. The sun which had been in my eyes so as not to see, had moved down past the tall trees. I finally saw Grandpa. He was at the cemetery. I hurried down the hay loft. Out the barn doors I ran. Across the pastures and the old

corn field., Nearly a mile I ran to be with him. .
I asked him why he was alone in the cemetery. He said, "see that new grave". That was an old friend. Well, he was and then he wasn't. Kinda used to be. He was jealous of my little farm. So much so that he lied on me every chance he got. I often prayed for his soul. I prayed for him to not let envy or greed corrupt his mind and soul. For him to know that hard work and a bank debt finally paid off gave me this farm . Job 16:20 *My friends scorn me: but mine eye poureth out tears unto God.*

He became so terrible that he even turned my family against me. They would not even help with any of the farm work, not even if they could take a share of the harvest. Job 19:14 *My kinsfolk have failed, and my familiar friends have forgotten me.* He became an awful person.

Grandpa said, "now there is an old saying that time heals all wounds." My friend now resting here finally did just that. You see he got his own farm. He got a fine mule. His chickens were some of the best. He was amazed how the bank would give him the money to buy it.

He went to church. He found Jesus as his personal savior. He turned over a new leaf. He even got my family to help me build a new barn, in just three days. He became a pleasant man. He became a giving man, generous to the church and community.

One day he came to me and told me how sorry and mean he had been to me. He said he felt so much regret. I asked him why the change of heart. He said first, I felt you praying for me. I went to church and meet your Jesus. He then said , the banker told me how I got my farm. How you co-signed for it. How you made payments even when I could not. Grand Pa said, " it's no matter, what are friends for"? John 15:13 Greater love hath no man than this, that a man lay down his life for his friends. He asked for my forgiveness, and I gave it. He said he could never repay me. Grand pa said, "Just be a friend".

Grandpa said yesterday I heard of his passing, Romans 12:21 *Be not overcome of evil, but overcome evil with good.* He had no burial plot, so I told his family to use one of mine. In his late life he became a special friend. A Christian friend that believed, accepted and love Jesus. We were both farmers ready to share brotherly love and God's love to all.

Today I just came to say "FAREWELL' 2 Corinthians 13:11 Finally, brethren, farewell. Be perfect, be of good comfort, be of one mind, live in peace; and the God of love and peace shall be with you.

We bowed our heads in silence. Grandpa said he may not hear my words, but for years he heard my heart. The birds sang a joyful song to us. We did not understand their words, but we understood their hearts.

Grandpa -Into the sunset

The sun rises and sets upon the old cornfield. Stories end and then they begin again. Only the Son and his story never ends till His return for the harvest. Be blessed and with God's aid we may plow this old cornfield again. Spread the seeds of Love, Joy and Charity to all mankind. We may all grow in different rows in the cornfield, but we are all the same until His harvest. . Matthew 13-30 **Let both grow together until the harvest: and in the time of harvest, I will say to the reapers, Gather ye together first the tares, and bind them in bundles to burn them: but gather the wheat into my barn.**

www.ingramcontent.com/pod-product-compliance
Lightning Source LLC
Chambersburg PA
CBHW071507070526
44578CB00001B/472